THE UNIVERSITY OF CALGARY

A PLACE OF
V·I·S·I·O·N

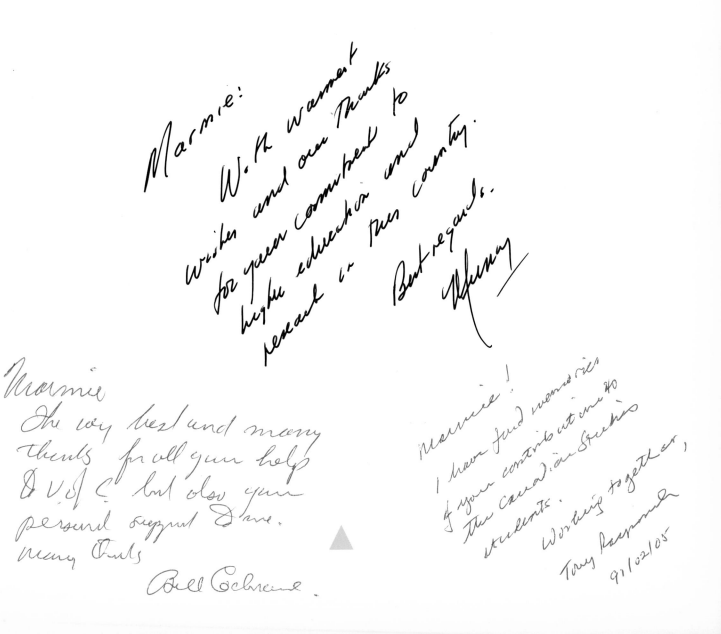

THE UNIVERSITY OF CALGARY

A PLACE OF
V·I·S·I·O·N

Text by Robert Bott
Photography by Roy Ooms

THE UNIVERSITY OF CALGARY PRESS

©1990 The University of Calgary. All rights reserved

ISBN 0-919813-85-2

University of Calgary Press
2500 University Drive NW
Calgary, Alberta, Canada T2N 1N4

Canadian Cataloguing in Publication Data
Bott, Robert, 1945 -
  The University of Calgary, a place of vision

  ISBN 0-919813-85-2

  1. University of Calgary — History. I. Title.
LE3.C32B67 1990   378.7123'38   C90-091666-4

Editor: Rodney Chapman
Design and Production: Kitty McLeod and Rob Melbourne/The Art Board
Photography: Roy Ooms/Lightworks Photography
Project Coordination: Stephen McElroy
Printing: The Jasper Printing Group Ltd.
Publisher: The University of Calgary Press in cooperation with
The Alumni Association of The University of Calgary

Printed in Canada

C · O · N · T · E · N · T · S

I·N·T·R·O·D·U·C·T·I·O·N

SOME OF MY FAVOURITE moments arrive subtly, even imperceptibly; slowly awakening into brilliant clarity. These entrancing moments happen rarely but are always savoured. Sometimes I'll be looking out my office window and observe an animated conversation between a student and professor, and something in that eager inquiring expression will trigger an explosion of insight into who and what we are at The University of Calgary.

It is my sincere hope this book will provide you with similar flashes of memory and recognition. These pages include the images and names of many who played a part in the development of The University of Calgary. There are others. Thanks to the achievements of all the members of the University family, we now celebrate twenty-five years of growth and success.

Throughout our time as an autonomous institution, the scope of the University has broadened from an early emphasis on teacher training to today's diverse curricula and a strong commitment to educate for life rather than employment. Our research efforts now reach into all facets of contemporary life, from the prevention of disease to the creation of cities, from prehistoric artifacts in the high Arctic to constellations in the cosmos. University of Calgary faculty, staff and students are making a difference through their scholarship, research and service in Alberta, in Canada and through-out the world.

Ours has become a diverse university, with faculty and students from many countries and cultures, with courses and programs that extend beyond the conventional boundaries of home and neighbourhood to school rooms in Nicaragua, clinics in Nepal and cathedrals in France.

The University of Calgary has evolved to become a cultural force within its home city and far beyond, through dance, music, drama and art, as well as the extensive scholarly and liter-ary works it has supported. It has also become an economic force of growing importance as Calgary's fourth-largest employer, with a regional economic impact approaching $500 million annually.

The University of Calgary is a complex organization which depends upon the energy, enthusiasm and cooperation of thousands of people. As members of a larger society, our highest commitment is to seek and to teach the truth, an ideal shared by universities for hundreds of years. As a beneficiary of those ancient traditions, we aspire to achieve the highest standards. As a young university, we are receptive to new fields of inquiry, new tech-niques of research, new methods of teaching, new ways of meeting public needs.

Ours is a story of accomplishment. I am proud of our history and I look forward to our future. Enjoy this book. Be part of our story.

Professor Murray Fraser
President and Vice-chancellor
The University of Calgary

C·H·R·O·N·O·L·O·G·Y

►**1905** Alberta becomes a province. The Alberta Normal School, for training primary and secondary teachers, established in Calgary.

►**1906** Premier A.C. Rutherford sponsors an act creating the University of Alberta. Land set aside in Rutherford's home riding of Strathcona.

►**1910** Act passed establishing Calgary College.

►**1912** Calgary College opens as a private post-secondary institution.

►**1913** Alberta Normal School renamed Calgary Normal School.

►**1914** A provincial commission recommends against giving Calgary College degree-granting powers.

►**1915** Calgary College closes.

►**1922** Calgary Normal School relocated onto campus of Institute of Technology and Art (now the Southern Alberta Institute of Technology and Alberta College of Art).

►**1940** Calgary Normal School and Institute of Technology and Art vacate SAIT campus to make room for war-time wireless training school.

►**1945** On returning to post-war SAIT campus, the Normal School becomes a southern extension of the U of A Faculty of Education.

►**1946** Citizens form the Calgary University Committee.

► **1956** First-year courses towards a Bachelor of Physical Education degree offered.

► **1957** First-year Bachelor of Science (Engineering) offered. Name changed to the University of Alberta in Calgary (UAC).

► **1958** F.C. Colborne, minister without portfolio, turns first sod for the present campus.

► **1959** Graduate-level studies offered; second-year Arts and Science courses offered, extended to third year in 1960.

► **1947** A.L. Doucette is appointed the first director of the Calgary Branch of the U of A. First two years of Bachelor of Education offered. Land set aside in Hounsfield Heights, southwest of SAIT, for eventual University site.

► **1950** Hounsfield Heights land exchanged for land along the old Banff Highway, site of present campus.

► **1951** Calgary University Committee sponsors public meeting to urge expansion of the Calgary Branch of the U of A. First year of Bachelor of Arts and Bachelor of Science offered.

► **1953** First-year Bachelor of Commerce offered.

► **1955** Calgary City Council passes a resolution transferring the Banff Highway property to the University.

► **1960** Malcolm G. Taylor appointed principal. The new campus opens with two buildings. Cosmic Ray Station in Banff also becomes part of UAC. McMahon Stadium opens.

► **1961** Name changed to University of Alberta, Calgary. Physical Education Building opens.

► **1962** Academic facilities expanded. Debut of Campus Patrol. Eighty acres north of campus designated for research facilities.

► **1963** First phase of Library opens in November. A student referendum is 78.5 per cent in favour of autonomy. Faculties of Education and Arts and Science established.

► **1964** Name changed again to University of Alberta at Calgary. H.S. (Herb) Armstrong appointed first president. Faculty of Graduate Studies established. Separate General Faculty Council created. Stage One (E Block) of Engineering Building opens. Football Dinos begin play. Grounds and greenhouse buildings erected.

► **1965** A policy decision sets the ultimate size of the University at 18,000, to be attained by 1986. Residence complex and Calgary Hall open. Science B and Meteorological Station completed. Faculty of Engineering established. Division of Continuing Education founded. On May 1, UAC is granted academic and financial autonomy.

FIRST COUNCIL OF THE FACULTY OF ENGINEERING
APRIL 1965

► **1966** Universities Act passed, creating The University of Calgary as an autonomous institution, effective April 1. Herb Armstrong is appointed first president and vice-chancellor; F.C. Manning appointed first chair of the Board of Governors; University Senate established. C.C. McLaurin elected chancellor. The Banff School of Fine Arts becomes affiliated with The University of Calgary. School of Social Work established. University Theatre and stage two of Science complex open. C and D blocks of Engineering completed. First informal meeting of Alumni Association. Mount Royal College and Medicine Hat College are affiliated with the U of C.

► **1967** First convocation of the autonomous University is held March 29; the first recipient of a degree, Doctor of The University of Calgary, is Prime Minister Lester B. Pearson. Ethel King-Shaw becomes first woman full professor and first woman elected to General Faculty Council. Faculties of Business and Fine Arts established. The University of Calgary receives a Grant of Arms. Students' Union Building (MacEwan Hall) opens. Education Building, B Block of Engineering, Kananaskis Centre laboratories and lodge, and extension of Calgary Hall completed.

►**1968** L.A. Thorssen appointed chair of Board of Governors. Compulsory class attendance eliminated. A Block of Engineering completed. Learned Societies meet at U of C.

►**1969** A.W.R. Carrothers named president. Social Sciences Building, Mathematical Sciences and Physical Plant completed. School of Nursing established.

►**1970** M.E. Jones appointed chair of Board of Governors. W.A. Friley elected chancellor. General Faculty Council renamed General Faculties Council. First students admitted to Faculty of Medicine. Science Theatres, Student Family Housing, Kananaskis Centre residences and extension of Physical Education complex completed.

►**1971** Four-year degree programs begin. Faculty of Environmental Design established. Spy Hill animal care facilities and Rothney Astrophysical Observatory completed.

►**1972** C.O. Nickle appointed chair of Board of Governors. Student representation on the General Faculties Council increased. Earth Sciences, Biological Sciences, Health Sciences Centre, Library Tower and link to Library Block completed. Indian Student University Program Service established (name changed to Native Student Services in 1974 and to Native Student Centre in 1978).

►**1973** Students' Union takes over management of MacEwan Hall.

►**1974** W.A. Cochrane named president. Muriel Kovitz elected chancellor. G.C. Swann appointed chair of Board of Governors. Master of Management Studies program launched (changed to Master of Business Administration in 1979). Gallagher Library of Geology and Geophysics opens.

►**1975** R.A. MacKimmie appointed chair of Board of Governors. Faculty of Law established. Schools of Physical Education, Nursing and Social Work become Faculties of Physical Education, Nursing and Social Welfare. Canadian Energy Research Institute founded. The Arctic Institute of North America relocated to U of C.

►**1976** Faculty of Arts and Science divided into Faculties of Science, Social Sciences, Humanities and the University College. Alumni Association incorporated. Day Care Centre opens.

►**1977** Division of Continuing Education renamed Faculty of Continuing Education. Banff School of Fine Arts separates from U of C to become autonomous institute, The Banff Centre for Continuing Education.

►**1978** Faculty of Business renamed Faculty of Management. The Nickle Arts Museum completed. Norman Wagner named president. J.L. Lebel elected chancellor. Space Science Research Group established.

►**1979** The Calgary Institute for the Humanities and the Canadian Institute of Resources Law established.

►**1980** First Alberta Oil Sands Technology and Research Authority (AOSTRA) professorship awarded to Ross Robinson, professor of Chemistry.

►**1981** The University College becomes Faculty of General Studies. Reeve Theatre and addition to Rothney Astrophysical Observatory completed. Archives policy adopted. The University of Calgary Press established.

►**1982** Brian Norford elected chancellor. Institute for Transportation Studies established. The U of C is selected as the 1988 Olympic Winter Games venue for the athletes' village and speed skating events.

►**1983** Three more residences are completed.

►**1984** A $17-million supercomputer is acquired. Office of Technology Transfer established. Robert Willson appointed chair of Board of Governors. MacKimmie Library named in honour of Ross Anderson MacKimmie.

►**1985** Scurfield Hall completed. Full-time MBA program offered. Calgary Hall renamed Craigie Hall.

►**1986** James Palmer elected chancellor. Canadian Institute for the Study of Law and the Family, the Walter Dinsdale Disability Information Service Centre of Canada, and the International Centre are established.

►**1987** Art Parkade, Glacier and Olympus residences, Heritage Medical Research Building, Olympic Oval, MacEwan Hall expansion and McMahon Stadium renovations completed.

►**1988** Winter Olympics in February brings athletes from around the world to the U of C. Murray Fraser named president. Enrolment frozen at about 16,000 full-time students. Co-operative Education Programme established. Consortium for Research on Elastic Wave Exploration Seismology (CREWES) established. Smoking banned in University buildings except in designated areas.

►**1989** Centre for Gifted Education established in the Faculty of Education. Institute for Space Research established. Faculty of Management proposal for Institute for Advanced Studies of Tourism is approved. U of C athletic teams win five national championships. Faculty of Social Welfare renamed Faculty of Social Work. Employment equity program adopted. The U of C is designated headquarters for the Canadian Network of Space Research, and a Network Centre of Excellence in six other areas. The Office of Technology Transfer becomes a University-owned management corporation, University Technologies International Inc.

►**1990** Richard Haskayne appointed chair of Board of Governors. David Smith elected chancellor. Total outside funding for research reaches $60 million from government and private-sector sources.

C · O · M · M · U · N · I · T · Y

THE UNIVERSITY OF CALGARY emerged from the needs and aspirations of citizens in the city and the surrounding areas of southern Alberta. But it took more than half a century for their vision to become reality.

The seeds were planted early. Education was highly valued by many of the settlers who moved west after completion of the Canadian Pacific Railway. As the first generation of children grew up, their parents demanded an institution of higher learning to complete their education.

The settlers realized the need for western universities. They could see that centres of knowledge were essential if they were to understand the many political, economic and technological revolutions — from socialism to new wheat strains to new modes of transportation — then under way. It was a heady time, marked by massive immigration and agricultural prosperity. Between 1901 and 1911, Calgary's population jumped roughly tenfold, from 4,400 to 43,700.

After Alberta became a province in 1905, a petition of 107 prominent Calgarians argued that if Edmonton obtained the capital, then the southern city should get the university. But Liberal Premier A.C. Rutherford, who also served as treasurer and education minister, overruled them and established the University of Alberta in his home riding of Strathcona (which became part of Edmonton in 1912).

In 1911, Calgary did get one post-secondary institution, Mount Royal College, sponsored by the Methodist Church. Under George W. Kirby as principal, it opened its doors in downtown Calgary on September 8, 1911. The community benefitted from the many cultural events sponsored by the College's Conservatory of Music and Speech Arts.

The Calgary university committee, led by an enterprising Ontario-born physician, Thomas Henry Blow, also persisted and raised private endowments for an institution officially called Calgary College but sometimes referred to locally as the University of Calgary. The first students enrolled in 1912, temporarily using the Central Park Library (now the Memorial Park branch of the Calgary Public Library). Despite entreaties from Calgary spokesmen such as future prime minister R.B. Bennett, the provincial government refused to grant Calgary College funding or degree-granting powers.

By 1913, Alberta's first great speculative boom was going bust, and the Great War was looming in Europe. Calgary College soon found itself short of both funds and students.

To determine the province's educational priorities — and to deal with the pleadings from Calgary — in 1914 the government appointed a commission made up of the university presidents from Saskatchewan, Toronto and Dalhousie. The commission recommended that the government support the U of A as the sole degree-granting institution for the province.

Calgary College closed in 1915. In its place, the city and province agreed to establish and fund the Institute of Technology and Art, which later became the Southern Alberta Institute of Technology (SAIT).

One of the more intriguing legacies of the original dream is the 160-acre campus design prepared by an English landscape architect named Dunington-Grubb in 1912. The campus was to be located west of the city in what is now Strathcona Heights. About the same time, architect Thomas Mawson prepared a grandiose city plan for Calgary, a copy of which is now preserved in the U of C Library's special collections.

The vision never died. But first there was war, hard times and the recurring argument whether a second provincial university would dilute scarce resources and merely create two inferior institutions.

The next concession to Calgary's demands was legislation in 1931 allowing Mount Royal College to offer first-year university courses in affiliation with the U of A — an arrangement that remained in place for twenty years. After that, however, depression and war again deferred debates about visionary investments.

Then, in 1945, thousands of returning soldiers wanted to resume their education. As well, it was not hard to foresee a coming baby boom. The government at that time decided to close Normal schools and consolidate the training of elementary and secondary school teachers under the U of A Faculty of Education.

Again, prominent citizens convened as the Calgary University Committee, chaired by William F. Reid and including F.G. Buchanan, Harry Francis, G.R. Gell and R.T. Alderman. They successfully blocked a proposal to transfer all teacher training to Edmonton, but were rebuffed in their renewed demands for a full-fledged university in Calgary.

Mount Royal College also put itself forward as the base from which a university could be built, but Premier Ernest Manning rejected all pleas. *"Consideration of this question has made it quite clear that the decentralization of University facilities inevitably must result in considerable duplication both in staff and equipment,"* he wrote to the committee in 1946. There was not enough money to go around.

However, the Faculty of Education became a foot in the university door. Sensing eventual victory, Calgary City Council set aside land southwest of SAIT for a university campus.

Initially, the Calgary extension offered the first two years toward a Bachelor of Education degree; the final year was taken in Edmonton. In 1946, it officially became the Calgary Branch of the U of A, and the following year A.L. Doucette was named its first director. About the same time, the Leduc oil discovery dramatically changed Alberta's economic prospects and considerably advanced the timetable for educational development.

Over the following decade, the Calgary Branch gradually expanded, and the U of A was utilized to capacity by the influx of post-war students. First-year Arts and Science courses were offered in Calgary in 1951 after another public meeting called by the Calgary University Committee put added pressure on politicians. First-year Commerce courses were added in 1953, Physical Education in 1956, and Engineering in 1957.

Calgary was growing rapidly — the population swelled from 90,000 in 1941 to 120,000 in 1951 and doubled to 250,000 by 1961 — and the demand for a university was stronger than ever. In 1950, City Council exchanged the designated lands near SAIT for the present site west of the old Banff Highway and in 1955 endorsed a resolution, introduced by Alderman Grant MacEwan, which turned that land over to the University.

The lobbying included advertisements on the tops of milk bottles urging students to enrol at the Calgary campus to force the province to move ahead. The students themselves chafed at the shortcomings of UAC, especially the inadequate library they shared with SAIT students.

Yielding at last to Calgary's long-denied requests, the government decided in 1958 to relocate UAC to the Banff Trail lands and make

19

it a full-fledged extension of the U of A. On a cool, sunny November 1st afternoon, Minister without Portfolio F.C. Colborne turned the first sod with a shovel that now rests in the University Archives.

Several hundred turned out for the ceremonies, which also included the first U of A convocation held in Calgary. *"This marks the beginning of a new life for us,"* Colborne said. *"Calgary is to become in every sense a university city."*

"Here, in these wind-swept hills, we'll see a dream become a reality," said Walter Johns, vice president of the U of A. Director Doucette added that the moment was *"a mark of new vigour for Calgary."*

Department of Public Works bulldozers flattened the hummocky prairie land the following summer. The first two buildings were the original Arts and Education (now Administration) and Science and Engineering (Science A). They might have represented unimaginative public-works architecture, but they were functional — a vast improvement over the pre-fabricated wooden buildings at SAIT — and they were built in record time.

Students who entered UAC in 1959 included some of the first who would receive bachelor degrees in Calgary, although those taking honours would still have to go to Edmonton for the fourth year. The first graduate students also registered that year, and Calgary, at last, was on its way to having a university of its own.

Classes moved from SAIT to the new campus in 1960. Soon thereafter, it became evident that there was one more battle to be fought. Students, faculty and community rallied together in a six-year campaign for autonomy.

The government and U of A authorities suggested Alberta could have a "California-style" university, a single institution with plural campuses. But Edmonton had a fifty-year head start, and the reality was that all important decisions at UAC required long-distance calls, sometimes-harrowing winter drives, or expensive plane rides. The system cost professors many days they could have used for research and teaching.

This was also a time when new universities were springing up across Canada. They included Carleton University in Ottawa (1957), York University in Toronto (1959), the University of Waterloo (1959), Trent University in Peterborough (1963), the University of Victoria

(1963) and the University of Regina (1967).

The students made their points boisterously. They staged boycotts, and they plastered the provincial legislature and the U of A president's car with autonomy bumper stickers. Their symbol was the Confederate flag, recalling a bloodier but less-successful southern secession drive. In a referendum in 1963, they voted 78.5 per cent in favour of separation.

The faculty was at least as frustrated, but somewhat more subtle in its attack. UAC academic staff simply began to take over functions supposedly reserved for the U of A General Faculty Council. Pressed by the faculty and students, the Board of Governors endorsed in January 1964 the establishment of separate faculty councils for Edmonton and Calgary and a coordinating council to deal with the government.

The government conceded *de facto* autonomy in most academic and financial affairs on May 1, 1965. Over many months of often-heated discussion, UAC faculty, administrators, board members and students contributed to shaping the legislation that would be needed to formally establish a separate university in Calgary.

A new Universities Act, passed by the legislature in the spring session of 1966, granted full autonomy to The University of Calgary, effective April 1. It is interesting to note that Mount Royal College also became a non-sectarian public institution on September 8 in the same year. The key elements of higher education in Calgary were in place at last. The pioneer vision was finally being realized.

Quite appropriately, it was the lieutenant-governor and former Calgary alderman and mayor, Grant MacEwan, who gave royal assent to the Universities Act.

The first U of C chancellor, Chief Justice C. Campbell McLaurin, made an invaluable contribution as he fought interference in the University by an old guard of political appointees. Later, he rallied support for the establishment of the Faculty of Law.

The first president, H.S. (Herb) Armstrong, felt that symbols were important for the new University, and wanted to recognize the city's Scottish heritage. (Calgary is a Gaelic word.) He arranged for the new University to receive its Coat of Arms from the Lord Lyon King of Arms in Edinburgh.

The University also adopted a Gaelic motto, *Mo shuile togam suas* (I will lift up mine eyes). This seemed particularly apt for scholars in a city where the vistas include big-sky prairies, soaring mountains, northern lights and the Chinook arch.

Armstrong also came up with a unique honorary degree, the Doctor of The University of Calgary (the DUC, sometimes called the "Doc" or "Duck"), first awarded in 1967 to Prime Minister Lester B. Pearson. Pearson was, in fact, the first recipient of a U of C degree.

By 1990, the University had a total of more than 52,000 alumni, of whom sixty-five per cent resided in Calgary and eighty per cent in Alberta. Some 5,600 held two U of C degrees, and 600 held three. The University's influence was evident throughout the community that gave birth to it.

''There is no question in my mind about the enthusiasm, interest and dedication of the members of the University community and, in turn, I have been overwhelmed and impressed by the respect, warmth and affection that the immediate community has for its University.... You ain't seen nothin' yet. I trust these may be

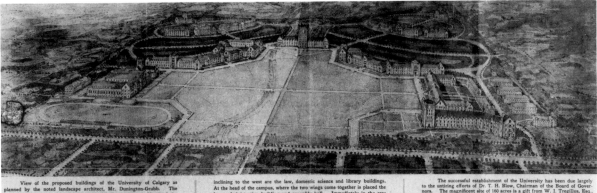

View of the proposed buildings of the University of Calgary as planned by the noted landscape architect, Mr. Dunington-Grubb. The stadium is seen in the south-west corner of the property. North of the stadium, the gymnasium, armory and chapel are grouped. North of this again come the medical building, museum and arts group. In the south-east corner are the agricultural and science buildings. North of these and inclining to the west are the law, domestic science and library buildings. At the head of the campus, where the two wings come together is placed the large administration building and assembly hall. Immediately in the rear is "Faculty Row" where the residences of the professors will be located. To the east of "Faculty Row" are the men's dormitories and to the west those for women students. The successful establishment of the University has been due largely to the untiring efforts of Dr. T. H. Blow, Chairman of the Board of Governors. The magnificent site of 160 acres is a gift from W. J. Tregillus, Esq., Secretary of the Board of Governors. The City of Calgary has shown its faith in the new enterprise by a gift of $150,000. To T. J. S. Skinner, Esq., falls the honor of endowing the first Chair. Among recent donations may be mentioned Lord Strathcona's promise of $25,000.

the watchwords of The University of Calgary as we move forward in partnership with a province and a people in transition.''

W.A. Cochrane
president, 1974-78

"My PhD supervisor suggested that I either give up singing or give up physics. There seemed more future in physics than in folk music, so that dictated my choice."

Derek Swinson
UAC PhD '65,
professor of Physics,
The University of New Mexico

D·I·V·E·R·S·I·T·Y

THE UNIVERSITY OF CALGARY was born at a time when students around the world were demanding greater participation in the life of their institutions. They wanted to be treated as adult citizens, rather than foot soldiers in an intellectual boot camp. They demanded a say in the organization and administration of their universities.

Southern Albertans, traditionally conservative and pragmatic people, always constituted more than eighty per cent of the student body. But they were not immune to the forces reshaping higher education.

Nor were they a homogeneous group. Each of the more than 52,000 students who received degrees in the first quarter century brought unique interests and talents to the University community. As it grew, the institution reflected this diversity.

There had been a Students' Council (or Education Undergraduate Society) since the founding of the Calgary Branch. But everyone commuted, and most were only there for a year

27

or two. The student newspaper was a mimeographed sheet.

The students who entered in 1959 knew they were laying the groundwork for a more permanent and distinct community. They established institutions, such as the **Gauntlet** newspaper, the **Tally Stick** yearbook and the April celebration of Bermuda Shorts Day, which became enduring features of campus life.

''Those first days focussed on establishing what a university was,'' recalls Maurice Yacowar (UAC BA '62), the founding editor of the **Gauntlet**, who went on to become an English professor, dean of academic affairs at Emily Carr College of Art and Design in Vancouver, and recipient of the 1986 Distinguished Alumni Award.

''In my first year, our last at the Tech, a compelling concern was to affirm we were not a high school,'' Yacowar says. *''So we grew beards and smoked pipes and skipped classes on principle.''*

Alan Arthur (UAC BA '62), another early **Gauntlet** editor who would later became a

professor of history at Brock University in St. Catharines, Ontario, launched Bermuda Shorts Day on April 1, 1960. The idea was to wear shorts and do silly things. The major event was a giant marble tournament.

Other institutions, such as a more active Students' Union and the weekly **Gauntlet**, took shape after classes moved to the dusty, wind-blown campus in the fall of 1960. Some of the first major controversies circled around the newspaper.

Founding editor Yacowar, caught up in the spirit of the times, thought it was part of his job to be provocative. He certainly was. The first brouhaha surrounded the issue for the week of November 11, 1960, which included a pacifist editorial by Yacowar questioning the wisdom of Remembrance Day poppy sales by the Royal Canadian Legion.

The Poppy Day editorial prompted a deluge of letters, telephone calls and public denunciations that flooded into the University offices, the newspaper and the Yacowar home. Principal Malcolm Taylor defused the situation with a gentle reprimand.

Campus life in those days was also enlivened by performances of the musicians who later formed the Irish Rovers. One of the early members was Derek Swinson (UAC PhD '65), a physics lecturer who received the first doctorate awarded for work done entirely at the Calgary campus. While his fellow musicians went on to fame and fortune after their hit song, "The Unicorn," Swinson became a professor of physics at The University of New Mexico.

For much of the first six years at the campus, the drive for autonomy was a central focus for student politicians. Scott Saville (UAC BA'64), later a Calgary lawyer and school trustee, was one of the key leaders in organizing the protests that ultimately led to independence.

Perhaps because they were allied in the autonomy struggle, students found the faculty and administration amenable to other demands. During a sit-in to protest closing hours at the Library, for example, the staff served cookies and soft drinks to the protestors.

As faculties and facilities expanded, students became more and more involved in shaping the campus. The opening of the Dining Centre and the first student housing in 1965 created a full-time community, and the Students' Union Building (later MacEwan Hall) in 1967 provided a focal point for student activities.

The Students' Union hired Frank Stoddard as its first full-time manager in 1962. Creating a centre of their own, the Students' Union Building, was a major undertaking. It summoned the managerial talents of the student body and became a symbol of what bright, young, educated people could achieve.

The elegant expansion of MacEwan Hall in the 1980s would later demonstrate the maturing of these seeds planted in the 1960s. The scope of the Students' Union widened greatly in 1968 when a system of vice presidents and commissions was established, providing the basis for the expansion of student self-government over the following seven years.

After a 1968 sit-in, the General Faculty Council (the name was later changed to General Faculties Council) first opened its doors to student observers and then accepted student and alumni representation. Compulsory class

attendance was also eliminated.

No compulsion was needed for one of the University's students, Madame Olga Valda, who received her BA in 1969 at the age of seventy-six, then believed to be the oldest graduate of any Canadian university. After enrolling as a special student in 1961, she became a familiar figure on campus, giving noon-hour ballet classes, contributing newspaper articles and coaching the basketball team in ballet moves. She died in 1973 and left her estate to the Students' Union, which used the funds to assist foster children in underprivileged countries.

Political debate reached a peak in the late 1960s when groups such as the U.S. Black Panthers were invited to visit. One of those arguing eloquently against "foreign revolutionaries" on campus was Ed Hamel-Schey, a satirical and often theatrical public speaker. After his death in 1974 at age thirty, a plaque was mounted in MacEwan Hall naming Hamel-Schey "Dean of Speaker's Corner."

Controversies also resulted in a "smash the **Gauntlet**" campaign in 1969. Critics forced a referendum that cut off financial support for the paper. An alternative called **The Medium** was published until the **Gauntlet** returned in September 1970.

Perhaps it was only coincidental that students found a new outlet for their opinions in 1969. Excavation for the Social Sciences Building unearthed "the Rock" which was relocated outside MacEwan Hall and became a magnet for political and other graffiti.

To reach the rapidly growing campus population, some student politicians tried innovative campaign tactics. Lamarr Stanford, running for student office in 1970, airdropped campaign literature. Unfortunately, some of the leaflets were off target and blew into Brentwood Shopping Centre. Stanford not only faced some legal charges, he also lost the election.

There were new signs of maturity. In 1970, students opened a crisis centre which operated until the City began offering similar services five years later. In 1971, Dinnie's Den became the first pub open to students on campus; it served only on Friday afternoons until the Alberta Liquor Control Board agreed to allow regular pub operations.

Student representation on the General Faculties Council increased from three to fourteen in 1972 and has subsequently risen to seventeen. This was also a significant year because, for the first time, there was no growth in the full-time student population, then standing at about 9,200.

In 1973, the Students' Union took over management of MacEwan Hall, at a saving to the University of nearly $100,000 in annual operating costs. Finances were becoming a major concern for the student body as the province limited funding increases in the mid-1970s. Protests and petitions escalated in 1977 when tuition fees were increased twenty-five per cent. Ten years later, 5,000 students blocked Crowchild Trail to protest funding cuts to universities.

A referendum in 1974 abolished the University Athletic Board and established the Campus Recreation Committee to administer funds for intramural activities. From the beginning of the athletic program, emphasis was placed on

providing fitness opportunities for all members of the University community, not just elite competitors.

The equality of women, already evident in many areas of campus life and advanced considerably by the establishment of a day-care centre in 1976, was affirmed by the election in the same year of Pat Ruby as the first woman president of the Students' Union.

The oil-and-gas boom in the late 1970s brought floods of new students — from Alberta, Canada and around the world — seeking opportunities in business, science and the professions. As the city became more cosmopolitan, so did the student body.

The role of Natives also grew after 1972, when the first Indian Student University Program Service was established. This became the Native Student Centre in 1978. By 1990 there were more than 120 Native graduates, including three doctorates, and more than 200 Native students were enrolled on campus.

Calgary's selection in 1981 as host of the 1988 Olympic Winter Games brought other changes and challenges. As the site of the athletes' village and the venue for speed skating, the University was transformed by the construction of $100-million worth of facilities — the Olympic Oval, Art Parkade, MacEwan Hall extension, expansion of Physical Education facilities, and additional residences.

During the Games themselves, thousands of students had to make major changes in their schedules and living arrangements to accommodate the extravaganza. Many participated as volunteers. The willingness of the University to alter its operations in order to make its facilities and expertise available to the Olympics was an invaluable contribution to the success of the Games. It was a first-rate example of cooperation between "town and gown."

Another display of athletic excellence came in 1989, when U of C teams achieved five national championships in intercollegiate competition — in men's and women's volleyball, women's basketball, men's swimming and football.

New waves of social concern, from fitness to environmentalism to women's and minority rights, were reflected on the campus of the 1980s and continue into the present. Students have taken the lead in many recycling programs and in contributions to food banks — without ignoring traditional events such as the Education Undergraduate Society's Winter Carnival.

A sampling of recent speakers on campus gives an indication of students' interests and concerns. They have included environmentalist David Suzuki, Lubicon Lake Cree Indian Chief Bernard Ominayak, External Affairs Minister Joe Clark, then Liberal leadership candidate Jean Chrétien, former ambassador Stephen Lewis, author Margaret Atwood, journalist Mike Duffy, and nuclear arms critic Helen Caldicott.

Another trend is evident in the composition of the student body itself. A growing proportion are taking time out for work or travel, and older students are becoming more common.

The Students' Union today has grown into a complex organization led by five commissions — Academic, External, Events, Finance and Executive Cabinet. It operates MacEwan Student Centre and provides services including a used bookstore, bar and restaurant, print shop, off-campus housing listings, travel board and yearbook cooperative. By 1990, it had thirty-five full-time staff.

In the University's first quarter century,

forty-seven per cent of the graduates were female, and by 1990 women accounted for nearly forty-nine per cent of enrolment. The median age of students had risen to almost twenty-three. While more than ninety per cent of the student body continued to be Albertans, the number of foreign visa students had risen to nearly six per cent. Students today come from every province and territory of Canada and from some eighty other countries.

"I don't think I've done anything in my life of which I'm prouder than the fact that I launched a paper that's still going, 30 years later.... Haven't read the Poppy Day editorial for many years. I don't doubt that it had more heat

than light and was too insensitive and virulent to excuse as Socratic. I was young."

Maurice Yacowar
UAC BA '62, founding editor of the Gauntlet

''If the University is to be in this world and of this world; if it is to perform its three missions (acquisition, transmission and application of knowledge); if it is to be concerned with values; if it is to serve a pluralist society replete with conflicting interests; if

it is to be concerned with the excitement of ensuring that society's reach exceeds its grasp, things are bound to happen in that stretch of former bald prairie known as the campus of The University of Calgary that will be heat generating and therefore disturbing.''

A.W.R. Carrothers
president, 1969-74

"As editor of the yearbook, I had several chats with (President) Herb Armstrong. He felt it was his duty to establish symbols for the new University. He was delighted to have an official Coat of Arms, and he made sure the University had corporate control over the use of its name.... He was irked that the teams were called the Dinosaurs. He felt they should be called the Wildcats. He wanted to drive a Buick Wildcat."

Patrick Tivy

BA '67, staff writer, Calgary Herald

▼

"Student activism and everything that goes with it — how you analyze policies and activities — has stayed with me and contributed to my work on the national stage. The most important thing that I learned was to be a free thinker. Those are

skills that are still with me. I still want to change the world.... The Faculty of Medicine is absolutely superb. I couldn't have gotten a better foundation for what I'm doing anywhere in Canada. I haven't found anything comparable."

Catherine Hankins
BA '71, MD '76, director, Centre for AIDS Studies, Montreal General Hospital

"We always seemed to be involved in pranks — whether setting someone's lunch on fire in the middle of a lecture; or removing all the toilet paper dispensers from the Arts Building and Calgary Hall and depositing them in the *Gauntlet* office.... More importantly, though, it was a time of tremendous change for me as an individual, both socially and intellectually. The bonds which grew from our common goals and shared experiences resulted in friendships which have lasted for twenty-five years."

Barry Lester

B.Sc. '69, M.Sc. '71 (Civil Engineering), partner Simpson Lester Goodrich, Calgary, designer of Olympic Oval, recipient of 1990 Distinguished Alumni Award

"I was quite thrilled when students chose my name for MacEwan Hall. I was there for both openings. It is pretty elegant today. I hadn't seen student enterprise like that — I was impressed by the fact that the students used it so completely."

Grant MacEwan

former alderman, lieutenant-governor and adjunct professor of History.

"I was your typical uninvolved working suburban housewife until I went back to the University. I realized that I could change things. I developed an orientation program to make life a little easier for the returning RN students, then became involved in

the Alumni Association, and I became far more involved in my professional association. It is a unique experience to go back as an adult student."

Marjorie Syms

BN '88

"They were on the verge of jackhammering the Rock to bits so they could load it onto trucks and get it out of here. Herman Hays and I said, 'Look, we'd like to keep it. . . .' And, of course, almost immediately somebody painted it."

Ian Duncan

former director of Campus Development

"Campus Recreation is a phenomenal operation. Twenty-five thousand people per week make use of these facilities. Over half of the student population takes part, which is triple the level of ten years ago. These are very user-friendly facilities."

Warren Veale
dean of Physical Education

''It was a very exciting time. There were some very gifted people in the faculty. I was very fortunate to be there when they were.... The University has changed Calgary a lot. It has allowed people to pursue their careers without leaving the city.''

Eric Friedenberg

BFA '72, musician

I·N·T·E·N·S·I·T·Y

THE FACULTIES ARE, QUITE LIT-
erally, the *abilities* of the University.
Not just administrative units, the
faculties define a university's special aptitudes and skills, the fields
in which it can offer great inten-
sity of knowledge and learning.

The senior faculty of The
University of Calgary is Education, which can trace its ancestry
back to the founding of the
Alberta Normal School in 1905. Its
Bachelor of Education programs
served as a taproot when the
young University sprouted and
flourished after the Calgary
Branch replaced the Calgary Normal School in 1945.

By 1959, there were also fledg-
ling faculties of Arts and Science,
Physical Education and Engineering. They were
all extensions of parent faculties at the U of A
in Edmonton, however, and initially offered
only first-year courses. In that year, graduate-
level studies were added, and planning began
for full undergraduate degree programs in addition to Education.

After the move to the new, two-building

campus in September 1960, there were 162 possible course choices — ninety-six in Arts and Science, forty-three in Education, twelve in Engineering and eleven in Physical Education — offered by seventy-five full-time teaching staff.

Like their students, these academic pioneers recognized that they had a rare opportunity to create new institutions and practices.

A key planning session was held during a weekend in January 1961 at the Banff School of Fine Arts. Under Principal Malcolm Taylor, they worked out the broad outlines for full degree programs and the facilities to house them.

Within a year, academic facilities were expanded to encompass complete general degree (three-year, non-honours) programs leading to the B.Ed., BA and B.Sc., the first two years of B.Comm. and B.Sc.(Engineering), as well as first-year courses in Nursing, Household Economics and Agriculture. Long-term

plans were developed for Engineering and Sciences.

The professors soon realized they could not flourish in the U of A's shadow. The Calgary academic staff voted for autonomy in 1963 and, a year later, established their own General Faculty Council, the central academic governing body of the University. By this time, the first UAC degrees were being awarded, and the campus was expanding at a phenomenal rate.

One of the most important faculties for a credible, independent university, Graduate Studies, was established in 1964 to oversee the work of all students seeking advanced degrees. The essential task of this faculty was to guarantee the standards of the University's graduate degrees.

James Hyne, a professor of Chemistry since 1959, was named the first dean of Graduate Studies in 1966. He would remain in that post for twenty-three years, the longest-serving dean.

A remarkably prescient long-range plan was drawn up by the faculties and administration in 1965 as the University neared academic and financial autonomy. Though technically "illegal" at the time, UAC General Faculty Council approved a curriculum for Engineering and chose Adam Neville as the first dean.

The Division of Continuing Education was founded in 1965 through the amalgamation of summer sessions and evening credit programs, formerly under the Faculty of Education, and non-credit courses offered by the Alberta Extension Department. It became the Faculty of Continuing Education in 1977 to reflect a greater involvement with the rest of the University community. By 1990, nearly 30,000 people a year were taking advantage of its many credit and non-credit courses. An information network linking disabled Canadians is also head-quartered at the U of C.

By the time full autonomy arrived in April 1966, the core faculties were in place, and plans were well advanced for a half-dozen new ones. The choices were a complex amalgam of provincial government requirements and demands from inside and outside the academic community. By the end of the year, Tim Tyler had been named as the first dean of Social Work (later renamed Social Welfare and more recently Social Work again), and the Board of Governors had approved faculties of Medicine and Business. The latter passed General Faculty Council by just one vote.

From 1966 to 1977, the University was affiliated with the Banff School of Fine Arts, which subsequently became an autonomous institute. A continuing affiliation of the U of C with Mount Royal College and Medicine Hat College also began in 1966.

In 1967, fine arts programs were reorganized into the Faculty of Fine Arts, the second such faculty in Canada.

Three deans — Tim Tyler in Social Work, William Cochrane in Medicine, and James Robinson in Business — faced formidable tasks as they had to plan facilities, design courses and recruit staff for their new faculties. In fact, the whole University was having a difficult time finding professors. The search was world-wide. One U of C advertisement in the **Times** of London showed a cartoon of a Neanderthal caveman next to the caption, "Professor? We need

your help...."

Cochrane's challenges included designing the innovative three-year Medicine program, only the second three-year program in Canada after McMaster University in Hamilton, Ontario, and planning the new Health Sciences Centre adjacent to Foothills Hospital. To complicate things, the funding was uncertain until the province announced a $25-million grant in 1969.

Shirley Good, the first dean of Nursing, faced similar challenges after the School of Nursing was established in 1969. It eventually would offer a four-year baccalaureate program, a two-year post-diploma baccalaureate and a two-year Master of Nursing program.

The next new faculty, Environmental Design, arose out of a recommendation of the Alberta Association of Architects in 1965, urging the creation of a school of architecture in the province. The Universities Coordinating Council subsequently suggested expanding such a school to include environmental studies. The Council thought the school should be located at the U of A in Edmonton, but the Alberta Universities Commission decided on Calgary.

William Perks, the first dean of Environmental Design, said one reason Calgary was chosen may have been the environmental expertise developed at the U of C by James Cragg and the scientists who worked with him at the Kananaskis Centre for Environmental Research.

Arts and Science expanded in 1971 with the adoption of four-year undergraduate degree programs, among the first in Canada, to replace the old system of three-year general degrees and a fourth year for honours degrees. It was already by far the largest faculty, accounting for more than half of University enrolment.

After a decade of dramatic growth, it was logical for the University to pause and take stock in the 1970s. Funding limitations and a slowdown in enrolment made this a practical necessity. A five-year plan adopted by the General Faculties Council in 1973 placed a moratorium on new programs, except Law.

Chancellor McLaurin and President Carrothers both wanted the University to have a law faculty, and there was a strong demand by the Calgary legal community for a first-class law library in the city. By the time John McLaren was named the first dean of Law in 1975, about $1 million had been raised from donations and government matching funds towards a law library. McLaren designed a relatively small faculty and placed a heavy emphasis on communications and negotiation skills. Not surprisingly, considering Calgary's role as Canada's oil capital, the faculty also developed considerable expertise in resource issues.

By the mid-1970s, the Faculty of Arts and Science had grown into an unwieldy administrative unit far larger than any other faculty. Finally, in 1976, the General Faculties Council voted to break it into four units — the faculties of Science, Humanities, Social Sciences and the University College. The University College, intended to oversee first-year and inter-disciplinary undergraduate programs, was renamed the Faculty of General Studies in 1981.

The following years saw many changes in programs but no additional faculties. The Master of Business Administration program, for

example, began as the Master of Management Studies in 1974 and became the MBA in 1979; initially available only on a part-time basis, it was offered to full-time students after the opening of Scurfield Hall in 1985. A PhD program in Management was introduced in 1990.

In 1977, approval was granted for a new doctoral program in Sociology and master's programs in Art, Dramatic Literature, Music Composition, Musicology and School Music. The Master of Nursing was first offered in 1979, and the Master of Communication Studies in 1982. Environmental Design expanded in 1980 to include Industrial Design, and Surveying Engineering was added to the Faculty of Engineering. The Co-operative Education Programme in 1988 allowed students to integrate studies and work experience.

Given Calgary's prominence as the head-office city for the Canadian oil industry, one might expect that faculties of Science, Management and Engineering would dominate the U of C's academic life. They certainly have drawn support and enrolment, especially during boom times, but other disciplines have also flourished.

Backed by the ample resources of the province's Heritage Trust Fund, the Faculty of Medicine has become internationally renowned for its education, research and science programs. Innovative programs have enhanced the reputations of faculties such as Law and Environmental Design.

But some of the biggest successes have been in fields such as Religious Studies. This department flourished within the Faculty of Humanities after the arrival of Peter Craigie in 1974. A charismatic teacher, Craigie had just taken office as vice president (academic) in 1985 when he died following a tragic highway accident. Calgary Hall was renamed Craigie Hall in his honour.

In 1988, another department member and former dean of Arts and Science, Terence Penelhum, professor emeritus of Religious Studies, received the prestigious Canada Council Molson Prize of $50,000 for outstanding lifetime achievement in the humanities and social sciences.

Entering the 1990s, one of the most striking features of academic life is the number of inter- and multi-disciplinary programs. The field of bio-mechanics, for example, now brings together the faculties of Medicine, Physical Education, Engineering and Science.

Environmental issues affect virtually every faculty, and computer applications have radically altered the way almost everyone works. And the original core faculty, Education, now embraces disciplines ranging from rehabilitation studies to special education for the gifted, while teleconferencing has extended its reach to teachers throughout the region.

More than five per cent of graduates in the University's first quarter century came from each of the faculties of Engineering, Graduate Studies, Management, Science and Social Sciences. The Faculty of Education accounted for twenty-four per cent of graduates.

"It is hard to imagine the city without the University. For a young institution, it has produced a remarkable number of community leaders. It is very much southern Alberta's University. We now have more than our share of authors and painters, and some pretty good journalists. The graduates have had a substantial impact on the community. We tend to overlook the role of the part-time student upgrading his or her education, but the University has been very responsive to this need. It is one reason the educational level is so high here."

Kevin Peterson

BA '72, publisher, Calgary Herald

"The idea of a Faculty of
Environmental Design was con-
ceived in the radical Sixties, born
and developed in the hopeful
Seventies, and matured in the
uncertain Eighties. By maturing,
there was a risk of profes-

sionalization, losing the innovative thrust. In the Eighties, I think the students tended to be more interested in their career prospects than in changing the world. Now there are signs that is changing again.''

William Perks
founding dean of the Faculty of Environmental Design

"We had a real problem attracting staff to an institution where all you could promise them was, quite literally, that they would be part of building the University. Sometimes you were attracting staff to a department

where there were only a few other faculty members, no support staff and few facilities."

Peter Krueger

professor of Chemistry, former vice president (academic) and provost

"Our Faculty of Humanities is less insular than those in many other universities. We have taken the view that it is important to join forces with the vocational parts of the University. We do a lot of teaching to people taking degrees

in other faculties. There is hardly any graduate who does not get some exposure to Humanities."
Ronald Bond
dean of Humanities

RELIEF GEOLOGIC MAP
OF
ALBERTA

LEGEND

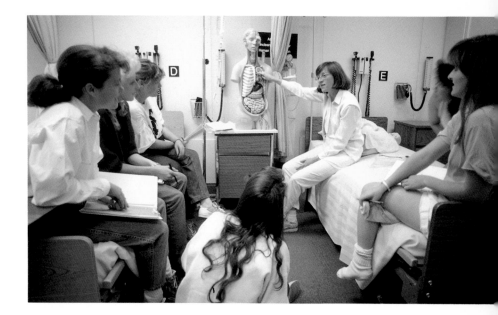

"The Institute of Resources Law is unique in Canada, and its reputation is international. Every year the institute attracts visitors from all over the world. Its work has provided a body of basic legal knowledge and analysis over the

past eleven years that was completely lacking in Canada. And its work has been quite influential in regard to government policy and legislative change."

Constance Hunt

dean of Law

''Undergraduate students learn existing knowledge; graduate students learn to uncover new knowledge. Graduate students in a university are apprentice scholars. They work closely with their supervisors to learn the personal

discipline that is part of doing research. The graduate school tests the students to their intellectual limits so that in their future endeavours they know what they are capable of accomplishing."

James Hyne

professor of Chemistry and former dean of Graduate Studies

"I am only too keenly aware of the pitfalls — and, if I may say so, pratfalls — which result when, eyes firmly fixed on the future, one stumbles into and over the obstacles which litter the path under our feet. I am equally

cognizant of the fact that serious problems are encountered if one is everlastingly concerned with the urgencies of the moment. Those who wear bifocal spectacles are aware of the difficulties.... Perhaps in this University, growing so rapidly, many of us are developing a permanent squint as a result of keeping one eye fixed on the immediate, while with the other we try to discern the future."

H.S. Armstrong
president, 1964-69

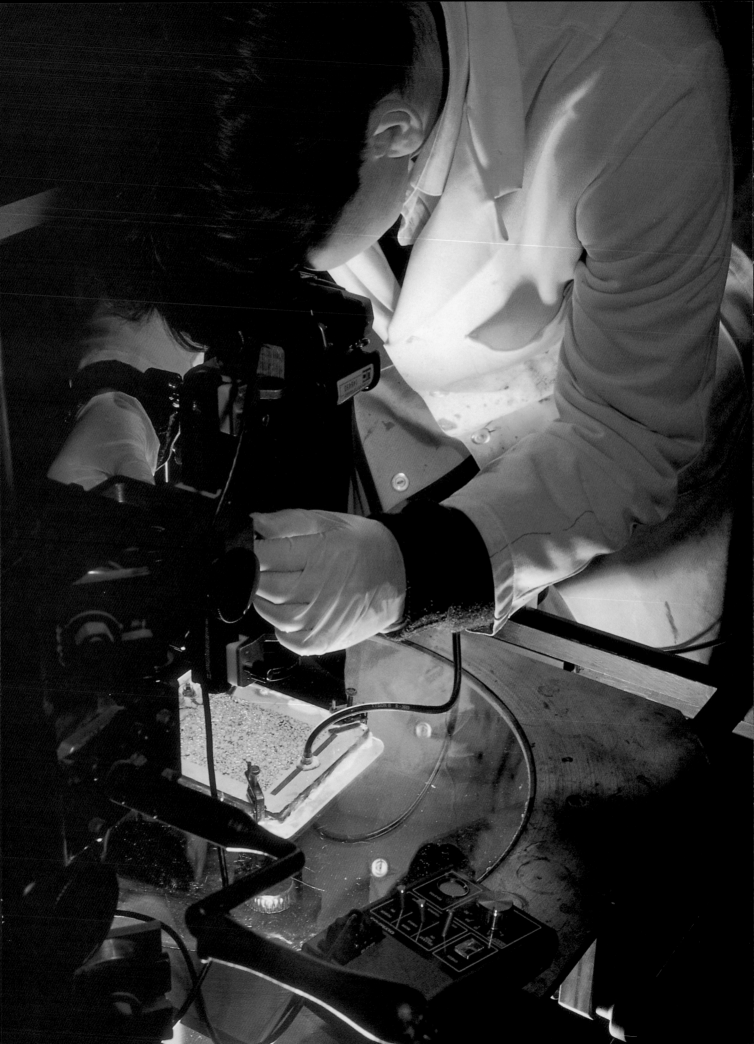

M·U·L·T·I·V·E·R·S·I·T·Y

THOUGH TEACHING IS FOREMOST among the University's tasks, research is the life-force, the source of renewal and growth. There must be time, money and facilities for research. Without such commitment, the University could not attract the best academic staff and graduate students. Nor could it participate fully in the advancement of the knowledge that it shares with students.

Perhaps the most important research component of the University is the Library. Virtually all research begins in the published record of humankind, which includes everything from ancient archives to the latest journal articles. The keys to this store of wealth are the talents of librarians, assisted today by powerful computers and vast databases. Beginning as a shared reading room at SAIT, the collection of five million items now ranks in the top half-dozen Canadian research libraries.

One of the first research facilities at the University was the Cosmic Ray Station on Sulphur Mountain near Banff, built for the International Geophysical Year in 1958 and taken over from the National Research Council in 1960. It was used by the first graduate students (in Physics) to pursue doctorates in Calgary. The station supervisor, Brian Wilson, went on to become a member of the Physics department, dean of Arts and Science, and later president of the University of Queensland in Australia.

A strong tradition of collaboration with industry and government scientists was established in 1962 when the City of Calgary set aside eighty acres north of the campus for research institutes. Among the first tenants were laboratories of the Alberta Oil and Gas Conservation Board and the Geological Survey of Canada.

Another type of industry-government-university research began in 1964 when Alberta Sulphur Research Limited was established within the Department of Chemistry. Over the years, it made possible many advances in the exploitation of a major Alberta resource, and it gave students and professors access to first-class laboratory facilities and real-world problems to tackle.

Research in every discipline advanced as more and more graduate students joined the University community. They had a powerful new tool at their disposal — the computer, now pervasive in every activity of the University. By the time autonomy arrived in 1966, an IBM computer was being used by researchers in fields such as anthropology, sociology and engineering.

One milepost for the University's research activities was its selection as the host campus in 1968 for the three-week annual gathering of the Learned Societies of Canada, a leading forum for the exchange and advancement of knowledge among academics.

While the Kananaskis Centre for Environmental Research served as a base for many biological and environmental studies, completion of the Spy Hill animal care facilities and the Rothney Astrophysical Observatory in 1971 opened up additional areas for researchers. In that year, the Engineering faculty also hosted 600 delegates at the Third Canadian Congress of Applied Mechanics.

In 1974, the Gallagher Library of Geology and Geophysics opened in the Earth Sciences Building; it was a personal gift from J.P. Gallagher, chairman of Dome Petroleum Limited, one of many generous donors who helped to make possible the Library's large collection of general and specialized works. Like the Law Library, the Canadian Literary Archives and the Canadian Architectural Archives, the Gallagher Library provided an important new resource for researchers.

The Canadian Energy Research Institute, located initially on campus in 1975 and later moved to the University Research Park, provided a centre for studies about the economics of energy. Meanwhile, it was decided to relocate to Calgary the Arctic Institute of North America, established in Montreal in 1945, and this opened up many important areas of study for U of C researchers.

Within faculties, research coalesced around such diverse bodies as the Calgary Institute for the Humanities, the Space Science Research Group, the Canadian Institute for Resources Law, and the Institute for Transportation

Studies.

Endowed chairs allowed academics to focus their research activities. The first of these at the U of C was the Killam Memorial Chair, endowed in 1967 by Dorothy J. Killam in memory of her late husband, Izaak Walton Killam.

The first holder of the Killam Chair was James Cragg, founding director of the Kananaskis Centre, a head of the Biology department, a vice president (academic) and emeritus professor of Environmental Sciences. Killam funds have also assisted hundreds of other scholars at the U of C.

The Office of Technology Transfer was established in 1984 to encourage the exchange of information between the University and industry. In 1989, this office became a University-owned management corporation, University Technologies International Inc. (UTI). One of its first products was a kit for detecting corrosion in pipelines, developed by three U of C researchers and a private-sector partner.

From 1985 to 1990, the University also housed a supercomputer, only the third such computer in Canada and the first available for public access. It helped to establish a continuing expertise in the latest computer techniques.

Following in the tradition of Alberta Sulphur Research Ltd., the Consortium for Research on Elastic Wave Exploration Seismology (CREWES) was set up in 1988 as an industry-university research unit.

Of fourteen networks selected in 1989 for the federal government's $240-million Networks of Centres of Excellence program, the U of C was designated headquarters for the Canadian Network of Space Research, and a Network Centre of Excellence in six other areas: Bacterial Diseases; Biotechnology for Insect Pest Management; Genetic Basis of Human Disease Innovations for Health Care; Microelectronic Devices, Circuits and Systems for Ultra Large Scale Intelligence; Neural Regeneration and Functional Recovery; and Respiratory Health.

By 1989, total outside funding for research had reached $60 million from government and private-sector sources. A study by the American organization Science Watch reported that the U of C had moved during the 1980s from fourteenth to twelfth place among Canadian universities on a scale measuring the impact of research papers.

One of the latest tools used by researchers is nuclear magnetic resonance spectroscopy, which allows researchers to look at the nuclei of atoms without harming the object under study. The NMR equipment cost more than $750,000 and opens up many areas of medical, agricultural and basic science research.

By the end of 1990, the number of endowed chairs and professorships at the U of C had grown to twenty-eight, ranging from Buddhist studies to geriatric medicine. In the future, these chairs and professorships are expected to become an increasingly important source of research support.

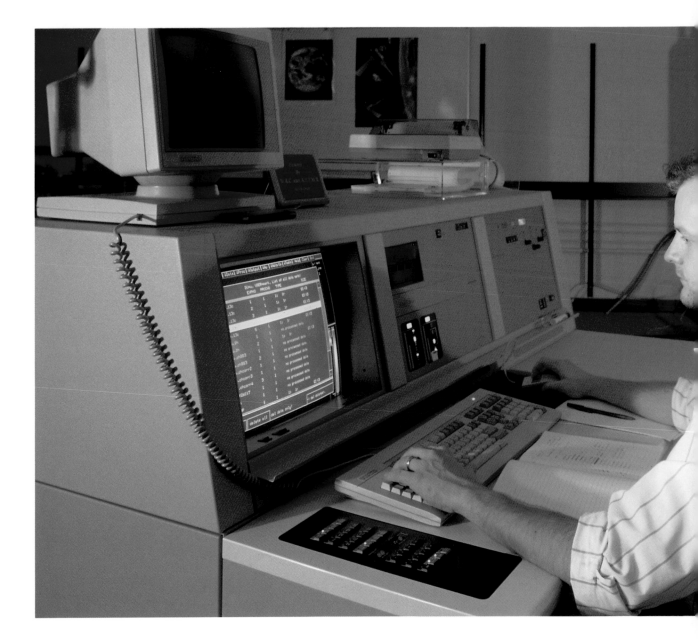

"Research is the *sine qua non* of the University. This is the only place in a free society where people can pursue ideas — do work without tangible results. Everything in this technological society started with research. And

you can't have 'pure' research in industry using shareholders' money, nor in government with taxpayers' money. In a society worth having, you need to know that you are going to be here tomorrow. The only way to achieve that is to allow research. It adds to our sense of humanity."

David Bercuson

professor of History, dean of Graduate Studies

"Because of the presence of the Foothills Medical Centre — including Tom Baker Cancer Centre, Foothills Hospital, Health Sciences Centre and the Heritage Medical Research Building — we are one of the major employers in

Calgary, so it has an economic spinoff. It is one of the centres in Canada of medical technology and science. It is one of the tertiary-care health establishments as well as a major educational centre. All of that together means that the citizens of southern Alberta and Calgary have enhanced health care available to them, and an awareness of the importance of preventative health care."

Bob Church

professor of Medical Biochemistry and Biological Sciences

''I think that a humanist has to have imagination, to be able to connect together ideas and attitudes that don't suggest their connections of themselves. The value of humanities is something which may not sound to everybody in our day and age like a positive thing at all. That value is that it makes you less confident of yourself in the sense that you are less confident that your immediate responses and reactions are the right ones. You go back and re-examine your assumptions.... I think this is very, very important. I think increasingly that in our concentration on the present and recent, what is close by, we are losing out on this.''

Terence Penelhum
professor of Religious Studies, former dean of Arts and Science

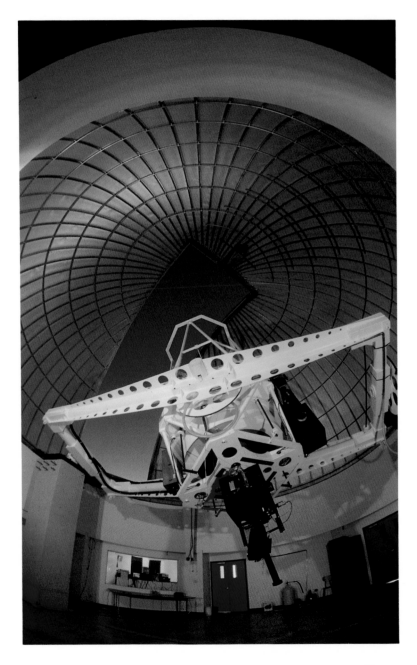

M·E·G·A·P·R·O·J·E·C·T

BUILDING AND OPERATING THE University of Calgary is a vast undertaking. In size, cost and complexity, it can be compared with the Alberta energy megaprojects of recent decades.

Unlike a government or corporation, The University of Calgary is not a pyramid of power emanating from the president at the top. The Board of Governors, General Faculties Council, Senate, provincial Department of Advanced Education, Universities Coordinating Council, Calgary City Council, Students' Union, Graduate Students' Association, Alumni Association, and others, all have varying influences on decisions.

Under the Universities Act, the Board of Governors has the ultimate powers, including the management and control of the University, its property and revenues. Direct control of academic matters rests with the General Faculties Council. The Senate acts as a bridge between the University and the community, is empowered to conduct inquiries, and acts as the "public conscience." The Senate also elects the chancellor and authorizes the conferring of honorary degrees.

The administration faced the challenges of incredibly rapid growth in the 1960s and abrupt slowdown in the 1970s, followed by renewed growth. It was often caught between the demands of students and faculty on the one hand and the provincial government on the

other. One of the more challenging years was 1975 when enrolment shot up 13.6 per cent, more than double the projected 5.1 per cent, while the province allowed only an 11 per cent rise in grants.

The physical face of the campus was shaped first by the Alberta Department of Public Works, whose bulldozers left a treeless plain which looked more like an airport than a campus. Howling in from the west, the wind churned up so much dust that the drum brakes of cars sometimes refused to function. Downwind neighbours were not impressed.

The first two buildings were plain and simple, typical government edifices of the 1950s. But more innovative architecture, imported from California for the original Library (now Library Block), was so unsuited to the Calgary climate that the outer cladding had to be torn off and replaced.

To create a more friendly and functional campus, a long-range development plan was prepared in the 1960s with the assistance of California planning consultant Louis De Monte. This plan, as developed and implemented by the University's own planners and by Walter Retzer's landscape crews, evolved into the comfortable, tree-lined campus of the 1990s.

An important part of the plan was to give the buildings some common architectural elements. The most notable feature was the use of pre-cast concrete finished with exposed flamingo quartz on the taller buildings.

What really transformed the campus was the landscape design of curving walks and thousands of trees and shrubs. The landscaping disguised some of the less-attractive architecture, ended the dust storms, created quiet spaces, and humanized the campus. The centrepiece was Swann Mall, named after former board chairman Gordon Swann.

Robert (Bob) Church, a professor of Medical Biochemistry who came from a local ranching family, helped landscaper Walter Retzer locate hundreds of trees which were given or sold to the University. A clamshell tree-moving machine, acquired in 1967, worked constantly from spring to fall.

The untitled sculpture by Vancouver artist

George Norris, commonly known as the "Prairie Chicken," was one of the first of many examples of public art to grace the campus; it has become a symbol for the Alumni Association and a popular outdoor gathering spot. Another favourite piece is the Zipper by Katie Ohe, a vertical, semi-kinetic chrome sculpture in the Science Theatres complex.

The second great challenge for planners, builders and landscapers came in the 1980s after Calgary was awarded the 1988 Winter Olympics. Nearly one-third of the developed area of the campus was dug up for new construction, and the deadlines simply had to be met.

Just accommodating the University's expanding activities, many of them highly specialized, was an enormous task. Each of these activities also required support services, ranging from clerical and secretarial support to sophisticated mechanical and electronic systems. Consider, for example, the plumbing and waste-disposal requirements for a chemical or biological laboratory.

The University today is virtually a city within a city. Its services include Caretaking, Security, Telecommunications, Physical Plant services, Identification Card Issuing, Lost and Found, Maintenance, Safety Office, Communications Media, Academic Computing Services, University Archives, Bookstore, Food Services, University Counselling Services, Faculty Club, Health Services, University Housing, Parking Services, Student Affairs, Registrar's and Controller's offices, University Printing Services, the U of C Press, McMahon Stadium, Public Affairs, Alumni Affairs, Devel-

opment (fund-raising), Purchasing, Central Stores, Shipping and Receiving. In addition, numerous secretarial and technical services are provided within faculties and departments.

"A university consists largely of people and depends on them above all for success in fulfilling its mission," said the University's Mission Statement in 1990. *"The University of Calgary is amongst Alberta's major employers, with over 1,800 academic and 2,350 non-academic staff. Our ambitions and our social role challenge us to foster an employment environment that is exemplary."*

The University has grown to more than forty buildings including seventeen academic buildings, a museum, two performance theatres, a superb physical education complex, and a students' union building. Its athletic facilities are considered the finest in Canada. Just in physical terms, it has certainly become a "megaproject."

By the end of the 1980s, the University directly provided the equivalent of about 4,700 full-time jobs and indirectly created or supported about 8,200 jobs. It was the city's fourth-largest employer, larger than any in the private sector. The U of C directly generated about $237 million in local business revenues annually and had a total economic impact estimated at close to $500 million.

Its very growth and success created a new set of problems for the administration and governing bodies. A study prepared by the University in 1987 found that provincial funding was failing to keep up with the University's growth and that the U of C was falling behind the per-student funding at other Alberta universities.

The temporary response to the funding shortfall was to place a ceiling on enrolment and, as a necessary consequence, to raise minimum admission requirements. Over the long term, however, such a policy would inhibit the ability to serve Albertans, whose vision gave birth to the University in the first place.

One option is to encourage donations. Since 1968, the Alberta Department of Advanced Education has fostered fund-raising through a series of matching grant programs. Though there have been some variations, these programs continue to the present.

Its own budget deficits apparently limit the capacity of the province to increase the annual operating grant, which accounts for more than eighty per cent of the University's operating revenues (approximately $180 million in 1990). As a result, the University increasingly has begun to look at other potential sources of sup-

port — alumni, private donors, the corporate sector — and to the revenue-producing potential of its internal resources. These sources alone cannot fund all the University's growth, but they can help substantially.

In 1990, the Legislative Assembly also amended the Universities Act to concentrate government control over the program content of the province's four universities. Many at the U of C were reminded of the autonomy struggle a quarter century before.

The acuteness of the financial crisis was evident late in the year when, for the first time in its history, the University announced it would be accepting no new full-time undergraduate students in the term beginning in January 1991. Eight hundred qualified applicants already had been turned down at the start of the fall term. Joy Calkin, vice president (academic), said funding cuts and overcrowding left the University with no alternative.

▼

"In both the joy and grief of human love, in both its presence and its loss, there may be a rich and deep quality to human life. Quality of this kind, I believe, is fundamental to a full human life, though it is quite beyond measurement. And quality of this kind may thrive in both poverty and prosperity, though either condition threatens such quality with its own peculiar kinds of dangers."
Peter Craigie (1938-1985)
professor of Religious Studies and vice president (academic)

"We've influenced, from inside and outside, how industry deals with environmental issues. With more than 350 graduates over two decades, we now have enough people in enough places that our philosophy has an

impact. And we can see that
growing exponentially."

Dixon Thompson

professor of Environmental Science

"Any landscape isn't right if it isn't pleasant, or you don't feel comfortable with it. And it just has to be something that you feel comfortable with, at peace with, and something you enjoy. Something you can relax with —

which, I think, is very important in a university setting. Students between classes, or professors or staff, may be under considerable stress, and hopefully they'll lose this sort of stress when they get outside into a landscape environment."

Walter Retzer
former manager of Grounds

''The international aspect we're seeing is going to be healthy for universities. It's going to make us reassess our understanding of humanity in a global sense, and that will be a starting point. There are pragmatic drives for this, at the political and economic level, but there is also a sincere effort to understand global problems, to understand people in other cultures, their beliefs. To try to match them intellectually and competitively will be very stimulating.''

Finley Campbell
professor of Geology, former vice president (priorities and planning)

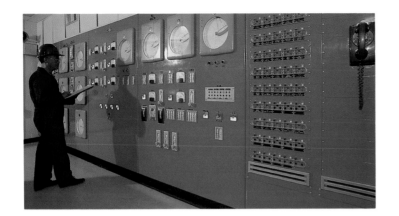

"I think we've done a masterful job. My feeling was that the calibre of our graduates would determine our reputation. Opening our doors to part-time students was a tremendous benefit. You have people for three hours a

week, and they're going out to
practice what they've learned.
There is a real dialogue. Our
students are movers and
shakers."
James Robinson
*professor and founding dean of
Management*

"I think The University of Calgary was really the forerunner of the western Canadian studies conferences which combined the disciplines of history, political science, economics and sociology among others. The annual volumes from those conferences have become important to the understanding of western Canada."
Anthony Rasporich
dean of Social Sciences

"The Faculty of Education has made significant contributions in trying to reach out and work with the Calgary school system. There is a close liaison. It has helped to put us on the cutting edge of educational thought. We now have a very modern, forward-thinking system....

The University has certainly helped to erode the popular notion of Calgary as an aggressive cow town and oil town. It gave cultural stability to a city that had been regarded as dynamic and volatile. It enabled Calgary to take a step forward in its urban development. As the University marched toward maturity, respectability and status, so did the city. The Olympics showed that."

Max Foran

B.Ed. '68, MA '70, PhD '81, historian and principal of Midnapore Elementary School

M·E·T·R·O·P·O·L·I·S

IT IS IMPOSSIBLE TO IMAGINE Calgary today without its University. Indeed, it is hard to believe the University is only a quarter century old. In most respects, the original vision has been realized.

The University is a product of the partnership forged between the people of Alberta and its provincial government. The give and take of debate throughout the years indeed demonstrates that democratic process can produce an institution of international stature.

The city's population has grown to 700,000, and more than forty-nine per cent of adults have post-secondary education. The University's presence gives solid backing to Calgary's claim to be a modern and internationally competitive metropolis. Scientists, doctors, lawyers, engineers, entrepreneurs, managers, writers, musicians and artists move here—or stay here—knowing

they can find academic resources, intellectual peers, and higher education for their children.

The University enriches the larger community in countless ways. Calgarians regularly attend concerts and plays and view exhibits at The Nickle Arts Museum. The media are enlivened by professors writing and speaking about ethics, history, politics, economics, arts and the environment. Members of the University community can be found in music groups, sports teams and volunteer activities throughout the city. Businesses are constantly calling for advice and help. U of C researchers have developed new medical devices, helped communities plan for growth and pioneered computerized instruction.

The majority of the U of C's more than 52,000 graduates also have stayed in southern Alberta, and they constitute a formidable network of influence. They include present and former cabinet ministers, the publisher of the **Calgary Herald**, the concertmaster of the Calgary Philharmonic Orchestra, prominent business executives, and twelve city school principals. A total of 149 U of C academic staff in 1990 held U of C degrees.

Faculty and alumni have also become active participants in the politics of the city, province and nation. In 1990, for example, the Member of Parliament for the constituency that included the campus was James Hawkes (M.Sc. '68), a professor of social welfare who also had been a president of the Students' Union at the Calgary Branch in 1953 and 1954. Another faculty member, Harvie Andre, represented Calgary Centre in Parliament in 1990. At the provincial level, Pat Black (B.Comm. '74) represented the riding of Calgary Foothills, and Dick Johnston (BA '66) was treasurer of Alberta.

After years of growth, however, the University still faced the double challenge of restrained budgets and increasing demands for services. *"It is clear that our next challenge will be one of consolidation and refinement,"* President Murray Fraser said in 1989. *"Continued success will result from identifying and building upon strengths. There will be difficult choices."*

A key part of this process was the drafting of a Mission Statement. The drafting began in 1989 and continued into 1990. The text offers an eloquent summary of the University's role as it enters its second quarter century:

The University of Calgary is a place of education and scholarly inquiry. Its mission is to seek truth and disseminate knowledge. Our aim is to pursue this mission with integrity for the benefit of the people of Alberta, Canada and the world.

Our university proudly shares the youth, energy and enterprise of the city and province with which we have grown.... Our history leads us to combine the best of long-established university traditions with the freshness, originality and independence of the Calgary environment. Our resources include the spirit of a frontier society and the worldwide heritage of cultures which have come together in our scholars, students and citizens.

As a university we are dedicated to the practice of scholarship which includes both teaching and research. Through research the university makes a direct contribution to society, and through teaching it prepares students to make their contribution. Students are bearers of knowledge for future generations and partners in discovery with their teachers. We offer to society the understanding and criticism of traditions and established structures, the advancement of science and technology, and the comprehension and development of human intellectual, artistic and physical endowments.

Our university is part of an increasingly interdependent system of colleges and universities in Alberta providing public access to a range of educational programs. We are committed to participating in this system cooperatively so as to serve the best interests of the people of Alberta. In our own programs we intend to balance breadth with excellence and to emphasize what we as a university can do best. In designing, managing and regulating our programs we assert the right of the university to independence from governmental direction. The university is responsible to the community at large and to the community's elected representatives, but the purposes of efficiency and enterprise, and above all the special role of intellectual and social leadership by which the university is defined, are threatened if our accountability is interpreted as subjection to political or bureaucratic control.

Liberal education in the arts and sciences is at the heart of our enterprise. We are proud also of our strengths in professional education, where our innovations include a three-year medical degree, the unification of architecture with other aspects of environmental design, a management program promoting entrepreneurship, an emphasis on outdoor pursuits in physical education, and a cooperative education program which is already opening career paths to students in the humanities and social sciences as well as the natural sciences and engineering. No university can achieve leadership in all fields. We already excel in some, and as we seek to excel in more, our choices will reflect the strengths we already have, the special characteristics and needs of our region, and the historical, geographical and economic factors on which we can build with advantage. In everything we do we expect to be measured by the highest standards of universities throughout the world.

Calgary is a young, growing and outward-looking city in a province and a nation which share those characteristics.... We welcome also the wealth of human ties and experience we derive from our multicultural population, both native and immigrant, and from the economic and cultural links which Calgary has with every part of the world.

The advancement of knowledge and understanding is a global enterprise. Accordingly we encourage national and international communication amongst scholars, we recruit academic and other staff with a view to making The University of Calgary a world-recognized centre of inquiry, and we aim to enrich the experience of our students by adding national and international dimensions to our student body and to the programs we design for them. The education we offer must prepare students to function in international as well as local contexts. We therefore foster fields of inquiry that deal with the distant as well as the local, the past as well as the present.

The needs of our students are central to our shaping of the University and our choice of directions. We aim to offer a sense of community, to address each student as an individual, to create a stimulating and encouraging environment for discovery, learning and personal development. The special features of this task include our suburban location, a large student population with only a small proportion resident on campus, and an increasing diversity amongst our students in age, experience, interests and expectations. Career change and lifelong education are becoming normal, and we are accommodating growing numbers of minority, mature, part-time, non-credit and other new categories of students. Our response must be flexible and innovative, combining the best of what we have established with the best that we can develop through new fields of inquiry, new methods of teaching, and new ways of meeting public needs.

"It is not an exaggeration to hold that universities, especially youthful ones such as The University of Calgary, must constantly rethink their roles for, as Adam said to Eve when they were expelled from the Garden,

'We live in times of transition.' ...I am hopeful that we will be able to find and defend a position enabling us as an institution to be a responsible corporate citizen. Yet, if universities are to fulfill their historic role of neutrality and independence from society, they must remain unencumbered and free to criticize and to comment and, I hope, to provide leadership to that society. Living with this tension is what makes universities constantly conscious both of their frailty and their greatness."

Norman Wagner
president, 1978-88

"The changing complex of modern
life requires that a far larger
proportion of young people receive
a higher education. Fortunately,
the increase in the national wealth
that results from more educated
people provides the tax base

necessary to finance education.
The more we invest in education,
the more we can afford to add to
the investment.''
Malcolm Taylor
*principal of the University of
Alberta, Calgary, 1960-64*

A·C·K·N·O·W·L·E·D·G·E·M·E·N·T·S

Special thanks are owed to the many persons who provided interviews, documents, photographs and editorial guidance for this project. The black-and-white photographs accompanying the Chronology and the Community chapter were all obtained from The University of Calgary Archives, with four exceptions: the left-hand photos on pages 10 and 13 are both from the Glenbow Archives, and the two photos on page 15 are from the Calgary Olympic Archives. In addition to the original colour photography of Roy Ooms, there are two colour photos provided by Alf Skraskins (upper left, page 70, and upper right, page 71), one by Mel Buschert (top, page 99) and one from the Olympic Archives (bottom, page 99). The author also wishes to thank the following persons for their assistance:

Ken Bendiktsen; David Bercuson; Horst Betz; Harvey Bliss; Susan Bloch-Nevitte; Ronald Bond; Sharon Boyle; Finley Campbell; Robert Church; William Cochrane; Melody Davies; Ian Duncan; Marianne Fedori; Darlene Field; Max Foran; Murray Fraser; Eric Friedenberg; Peter Glockner; Earl Guy; Catherine Hankins; Lois Hargrave; Constance Hunt; James Hyne; Dianne Jorgenson; Ethel King-Shaw; Peter Krueger; Jean Langdon; Grant MacEwan; Terence Penelhum; William Perks; Kevin Peterson; Anthony Rasporich; Beth Raugust; John Rayner; Walter Retzer; John Roberts; James Robinson; Pat Ruby; Donald Smith; Ted Sullivan; Derek Swinson; Marjorie Syms; Jean Tener; Fred Terentiuk; Dixon Thompson; Patrick Tivy; Tim Tyler; Warren Veale; Judy Widas; William Zwerman.